KEVIN CROSSLEY-HOLLAND writes poems, translates from Anglo-Saxon, reworks traditional tales and writes prizewinning historical fiction for children. He has collaborated with the artists Norman Ackroyd and James Dodds and many composers including Nicola LeFanu, Bernard Hughes and Bob Chilcott. He is an Honorary Fellow of St Edmund Hall, Oxford, Fellow of the Royal Society of Literature, and President of the School Library Association.

Kevin Crossley-Holland

THE BREAKING
HOUR

ENITHARMON PRESS

First published in 2015
by Enitharmon Press
10 Bury Place
London WC1A 2JL

www.enitharmon.co.uk

Distributed in the UK by
Central Books
99 Wallis Road
London E9 5LN

Distributed in the USA and Canada by
Independent Publishers Group
814 North Franklin Street
Chicago, IL 60610
USA
www.ipgbook.com

ISBN: 978-1-910392-09-6

ISBN: 978-1-910392-22-5 (signed limited edition of 35 hardback copies,
clothbound at The Fine Book Bindery)

Enitharmon Press gratefully acknowledges the financial support of
Arts Council England, through Grants for the Arts.

Individuals contribute to sustain the Press through the
Enitharmon Friends Scheme. We are deeply grateful to all Friends,
particularly our Patrons: Colin Beer, Sean O'Connor and those
who wished to remain anonymous.

British Library Cataloguing-in-Publication Data.
A catalogue record for this book is available
from the British Library.

Designed in Albertina by Libanus Press
and printed in England by
Short Run Press

ACKNOWLEDGEMENTS

'Trespasses' was first printed in *Ambit*, 'What She Promises' in *The Author* and *The School Librarian*, 'Words' in *The Dark Horse*, 'Harald in Byzantium' in *Long Poem Magazine*, 'Wintering Grounds' in *Norfolk Living*, 'Nelson Country' (under the title 'Calling') in *The Rialto*, 'Sea-Dew' in *Temenos Academy Review*, 'Boyhood, 'The Syrian Goddess' and 'Translations' in *Theology*, 'A Quiet Mind', 'Lifelines' and 'The Remit of Love' in *Urthona*.

The Poetry Society and Norwegian Embassy commissioned the translations of 'Snow and Spruce Forest' and 'North'; the former was wrapped around the base of the Trafalgar Square Christmas tree. 'A Prayer for Saint Edmund' was written at the invitation of the parish of Hoxne in Suffolk and, in a setting by Jonathan Baker, first performed in November 2013. My thanks to Magali Lelong and Stein Iversen for their guidance on my translations from French and Norwegian.

'Miriam' and 'Clarification' were first published in *Attraction Water* (Toppesfield: The Happy Dragons' Press, New Garland No. 15, 2011). 'The Roses of Camon' first appeared in *A Garland for Helen* (privately printed, 2013).

CONTENTS

THE BREAKING HOUR

BOYHOOD

1

Let me begin again.

No, not embedded in the womb
but with this boy in sensible grey shorts
the way he walks no distance
between actual and numinous.

So eager, so open-eyed

so involved with story
but in Chesterton's white light
unbothered by what was or will be,
mythology, metaphor.

Let him recover me.

2

Above me the chalk cross soared
from our doorstep to heaven.
I knew it always had,
and always would.

Below me the train steaming
from where to where across the blue Vale
coughed and paused
at Monks Risborough and Whiteleaf Halt.

Still so uncurious,
yet so soon to set out
wyde in this world wondres to here.

3

'Do you want to remember
here and now?'

In my bath I squirmed round.
'What do you mean? How?'

'By deciding to. By wanting to so much
there's nothing in your head, your heart
but this steamed-up room,
look, this laundry-box, your yellow towel,
you, me, these words…'

I stood up and dried myself, properly.
Mindful, I walked out of Eden.

TRANSLATIONS

Scan

As when some steepling wave
seems arrested, or cumuli
draw close, couple and configure,
we glimpse this dream made flesh,
half-smiling, left hand raised.
And each of us comes face to face
with innocence, manifest,
ineffable unearthly bliss
before we compromise it.

Before the Breaking Hour

Love-knot, dovetail, harvest bow:
they've waited all their lives for you
and wish you everything they want.
Their sit-at-home, their rope-dancer,
their hyphen and fuse and chord:
now, before the breaking hour,
vital image, simplifying word.

Cradle

Not woven from purple rushes
and, daubed with slime and pitch,
left to bob among flags.
Not lined with watercolour silks
– gifts of the Good Fairies.
Nothing less than this soft rain

so still through the watches,
each sweet drop giving voice
to earth and grass, leaf, roof,
pane, and yes, whatsoever is.

COMMUNION

No, I never commune with my ancestors
before breakfast. But the roneo'd foolscap
pages of *Lore and Legend of Flintshire,*
musty yet tart, opened the creaking door
to my father's study; and this afternoon,
 while rummaging for two-inch nails
in a cigar-box stuffed with nothing but screws,
I encountered my grandfather Frank
gazing at me over his half-moons,
beginning a homily. At certain times
my younger son does look uncommonly
like him. And just now I'm well aware
of a whole blood-company of crooks,
antiquarians, ministers and warriors
standing behind me, awaiting the firstborn
and hardwon, all of them silent, all attentive.

MIRIAM

I have entered the garden of superstition
where it is unwise to gaze at moon jellyfish
or the undersides of toadstools
and a scuff on the bracelet bearing your name
may be no less a portent
than a crack in the teacup or temple.

The language of yes and Fortune herself
are not so much inevitable as invited.
I am in league with prime numbers,
hagstones and anagrams – even the lottery –
and potter about, smelling lavender.
I consort only with whatever is propitious.

Each day I am learning more
about longing and the longed for,
attending to my Hebrew.
I have met your half-sisters,
Maria and Mariam, Minnie, Maire,
and I kneel before the Virgin.

Etymology has its limitations.
Your name like all names grows in sound:
the humming of bees, vowels cheeping,
and that capricious r, rolled in the throat
or butterfly light, fluttering on the tip
of the tongue. That's the sum of it.

THE REMIT OF LOVE

As the weather worsens
each remission is more beautiful.

Daughter, we abandoned our palisade
defended by marram
and launched ourselves from dunes
always eroding.
And when we crossed sodden sand
quick beneath our feet
you pointed to a shape:

a lump-and-dazzle
perhaps a couple of hundred yards out,
you can never be certain in this razor light.

At Brancaster, where the prospect is bleak
and flint waves angled in
as usual from north-east,
steepling and falling on themselves,
you waded through the shallows,
and there you stood, attentive
as a heron, while chill water
scalloped shingle under your heels and toes;

and I supposed
you might be thinking of what you knew about her,
her mother, her father,
reduced to this blob dipping and rising;
half-aware already of deep waters,
your own longing
to salvage and redeem.

I saw you both: two young girls, two daughters
caught on either side of time
– and like a bright lance unerring,
piercing the breakers,
the remit of love.

L'ÉCOLE DES BEAUX-ARTS

From the wicker box
their father selects a little twist of paper
and lobs it
into the bowl of water
in front of his curious sons and daughters
Now the majestic Japanese flower
unfurls and opens
instantaneous lotus
in its coat of many colours
and the children
hold their breath
captivated
Though years may pass
this flower can never fade
this all-of-a-sudden flower
made for them
in just a moment
before their eyes

translated from the French of Jacques Prévert

TRESPASSES

Often we inspected our father's beds,
each ruled with drills straight as staves,

our mother's rockery stitched with Alpines
airlifted home, wrapped in damp muslin,

but it was the gooseberries behind the old shed
claimed us and blood-blushed our wrists.

Between two rows we scooped our hidey-hole
and topped and tailed with our thumb-nails,

and that was where we welcomed Bruce
with open arms after the massacre.

He planted his victims like a regular gardener
only to turn his back and ignore them,

but later suffered a Buff Orpington
around his bull neck by way of punishment.

'He'll never do it again. He won't, will you?'
Bruce whisked his tail, he rapped it,

his dark eyes gleamed, and on our knees
beside our bunk three times we murmured

the Lord's Prayer, then absolved him
in the blue hour and slipped his lead.

Silent as death, we slunk away,
past the shed, past the morgue,

then tore up Whiteleaf Hill, rejoicing.

WATER-SPIRIT

Wimblington is where you fell out of the sky
not at first like a sweet shower on a changeable day.
I'm thinking of the way like a shining spear or javelin
a waterfall can spout quite clear of a cliff, her force
for a moment little less than gravity, before she arcs
above a valley, graceful and loosening, and drifts
to the supple floor, an umbrella golden, many-coloured.
Water-spirit, my own daughter, rising, riding,
I see you falling, falling and laughing. Elementary.

MEMINI

In a spring glade, eyes half-closed, music-making
– that's where I located you,
in the ancient beech woods. I stood before you, shaking.

You gazed at me. No, not 'at'; you gazed 'through'.
Why have you come so far?
What more do you think you need to know?

Tongue-tied, I stood. Come so far, now so near.
You told me then,
as you often did, only to dare

to ask myself questions for my own star
to lead me through fire, flood.
But home again, if this is home, my words turn sour,

I'm still infected in my head and seething blood.
Not because you did not
– so few men of your class or time ever stood

naked – but because you never once uttered
the words I longed to hear,
never understood what I believe: that what

is neither written by hand nor heard by ear
is never wholly so.
Father, father. Back again, back, always, everywhere.

You close your eyes, gentle and smiling, sky-blue,
and incline to your Welsh harp.
Remember who you are. Memini. Who are you?

KIM'S GAME: FIRST VARIATION

Begin with a dozen items, their order determined
only by pulse and music. The sound of night-rain,
very softly falling. The smell of chloroform,
and a chess-set fashioned from ivory and light.
That secret I can never share, and the stench
of my own fear. The high jinks of the first swallow.
A Liberty handkerchief (circa 1976),
and the aroma of wild strawberries. The scent
of a baby. Crunch-crunch of snow underfoot.
That fatal first kiss ... Well, I'm keeping one
to myself for the moment. This is my game now.

I knew what was to come after the cake
and candles and the snaps with the Brownie:
that dreadful covered tray ... My throat grew dry.
So why am I still competing, and with whom
(e.g. the Grim Reaper, Dr Alzheimer, no-one)?
Gut has guided me, and I see all five senses
are represented, though I've this sense sometimes
of something beyond sense. No ideas but
in things, true, but in things not only presences,
absences too. Please go back to the beginning.
Would you care to adopt any of my items?

PASSAGES

Che faro . . .

Not the flap-flap and boom of a marquee
or the raucous joy of wild geese returning,
not leaf-scrape and rattle or some hailer
broadcasting from other worlds,
not even a single insistent fly
weaving around a clammy wrist . . .

*

In the chill enclosure – its only sound
no-sound, the pressure of it,
wanting even the breath and beat of being –
white mist lifted, dipped,
and the wraiths listened . . .

*

When Orpheus played and sang
he gave them back their time,
gave them memory . . .

*

And that he sang as he did,
standing where the passage widened
and admitted a shaft of pale daylight,

as if for the first time he understood
how he must find in grief growth
and whatever's fruitful:
so whole-hearted,
so generous, and that only made
his desolation more unbearable . . .

LIFELINES

Grey-green thunderhead. So tell me,
who scrapped it because of this fissure?
A lookalike with a stubborn jaw, high cheekbones
and an engaging chuckle?

This lip of a samite dish,
did it slip through the fingers of some Norfolk lass
harassed and ravished by a Dalmatian horseman
in his cups?

And this dividing-bowl; this dandy;
this slim-hipped girl; this neck of a nacreous bottle;
this little finger…

Between outrageous thistles
and patches of vetch, yellow-and-purple, beneath
our springing soles, an inch deep, a yard,
never much more than that, they're all so much
closer than we think.

Closer and warmer,
immune to illness, scornful of the shining edge,
lying in wait like rolling fairground pennies,
lodged across the lines between who they were
and might have been.

Yes, we squinted
at the same sun and were assailed
by the same bitter squalls. Bleached
by salt, we lived within earshot
of the same ocean.

But who were they,
these men and women with their litters of children
and scrawny herds of animals,
on their way between worlds,
and how are we to understand them?
What did they mean?

This pierced coin,
is it an affirmation of Empire,
a talisman, a love token, or simply
the difference between a full stomach
and going to bed hungry?

Birth and hope,
maddening passion, each of our stepping-stones
attended by rituals, as we hasten
towards the Four Last Things:
the very abstracts that unite us
separate us.

And yet, sometimes
– times between times – when the fret
lifts and the world grows wholly wonderful,
we believe for a moment that we've levelled
our gaze and are singing in unison,

and only our own doubt
and sense of difference dates us.
Look! They have not gone away.
Not one of them. It is we who leave them;
and now all we can do is love and grieve them.

Warham Camp and Branodunum

A PRAYER TO SAINT EDMUND

Hwaer eart Þu?
Hwaer eart Þu nu gefera?
Hwaer?

Where are you?
My friend, where are you now?
Where?

Your companions kept calling
and, between the wolf's paws,
your head answered, 'Here! Here! Here!'

Now, in our season,
people of Hoxne and East Anglia,
we call for you, Holy Edmund.

Eadmund se eadiga,
Eastengla cyning,
snotor and wurðfull.

Blessed Edmund,
King of the East Angles,
wise and honourable.

Taunted and whipped,
roped to a tree, your body bristling.
Your head lopped off.

You suffered and died for us
and now, in our season,
we call from the darkness.

Edmund, Edmund, search out
and enter each head, each heart.
Find us, and guide us.

Hwaer eart Þu?
Hwaer eart Þu nu gefera?
Hwaer?

My friend, where are you now?
Where?
Dear friend, find us.

HARALD IN BYZANTIUM

The eyes of my women
are dawn-grey, dawn-blue.
Here, they are black stars,

and a little painted fingernail
achieves more than a northern
screech or pitchfork.

In a climate cold and wet
there's very little blaze,
not even much smoulder.

I have resolved to stay
in Miklagard a little longer.

*

In this they are alike.
Eye-proud, word-proud.
They stand taller
than they are.
They lie proud.
Their birthright.
Dark Madonnas, pale goddesses,
on this side of the rainbow bridge.

*

My fjord winds to a turf-roof
and the glacier's blue teeth.
I can hear the quernstone
grinding the salt in the northern sea.

Your smooth-skinned channel slides
between bluffs. Even when the water
is pink, violet, you can see her depths,
her rounded white rocks shimmering.
I do not know where you are taking me
but I have no choice, only an imperative.

*

Loose gravel grits its teeth,
then packs and shoulders down.
Frazil ice congeals.
Wolf-wind from the east
leaps over White Hill, snarling.
It bays at the bruised moon.
Young men must sometimes choose
hardship because it is hardship.

*

I've heard of a Varangian grown too old
to raise shield or scramasax. One autumn
a Muslim girl with downy cheeks
lit his braziers. Come winter
he married her, and he settled
in Trebizond, but…

*

… welcomed my dragon-prow,
waving from their swarm of dugouts
or cobles or knars or whatever they call them.

Sails blue as promises, pink as flamingos
and green and bitter as kelp.
I was not born yesterday.
Sweet today is often sour tomorrow.

*

Like the High One, Thought will perch
on my left shoulder, Memory on my right.
Each is the child of the other.

What choice have I? Can a man be free?
If not to change his fate, then at least
to drink and laugh and to deride it?

*

What was it my English *scop* sang?
'Amber and jet. Pearl, swansdown.
Woodsmoke, tart and sweet. Sopping
clouds, old habits. Dear unknowings.'

Yes, where's the true tip of the spear
when grapes and figs grow on the terrace?
Men here are pampered and impenitent.
Uncertainty, there's the best mulch.

I ask not for sight but to learn how to see.
Give me high latitudes to grow spirit-fruit.

*

Garthar, Garthar,
not here, not there
but in between.

In her forests
she will grant you
nothing
but nettles, thorns, teeth,
night eyes shining.
There's no escape,
you cannot withdraw.

Her hair, wild black,
a dozen times
she winds it around you . . .

*

Some men I know dream dreams
that step with them through their lives
– light and dark shadows.

My life-companions are the nine runes
chanted over my cradle:
green, storm, blade,
wild, stone, between, king,
bone, paradise.

They spell my story,
my fate if I can riddle them.

*

Slingstones have their limitations.
With my battering-ram I'll breach
those soaring walls. And I will dispose
of that Armenian lout, Gyrgir . . .
I will do this, I will do that
and that and that. But who can say
whether you will lie with me
shining in your cocoon of Jewish silks?

*

. . . gives me
elbows and knees, the plates
of my shoulder-bones,
gives me back
the thud of my heart.

*

I become breathless. I am tormented.
I would trade days
to feel again on my palms
the weight of your perfect breasts,
to hear once more the way
you sweet-mouthed my name.

*

. . . but if I take what you will not give . . .

*

The delicate contraption of your right ankle,
the downy crooks of your arms,
your swan-neck.

               Dear Gods,
I who will rule
the whole northern world . . .
My head is thumping. My heart spinning.

        *

Blood scab blotch rust.
Hard as your heart,
locked as my fist.

Here, I'll skin this heartstone
with hammered gold and return it…
No! I'll roast it

so I can see right through it.
I'll crush it between my palms,
soften and remould it.

        *

Ruler and slave,
              ice and flame,
was, will be:

whatever I am,
              wherever I am,
I am between.

One man threshing
                    in this web
between despair
                    and ecstasy.

                    *

Let the gods grow old.
Let them become mumbling imbeciles.
Let them become incontinent.

Grant me one night
in your apple-garden,
forever young,

and I will outgod the gods.

IN HAGIA SOPHIA

1 *Varangian Mercenary*

What if there's no afterlife, least not
for the likes of me, and after death
nothing but afterdeath? So what!

Pff! I'm pickled as a herring.
Since when did the dead ever go away?
We live in the presence of our ancestors.

Soon enough she'll get the better
of my rotten body – that's up to fate –
but I'll not have Time outstrip me.

Here now. On this shining ledge
I'll score my runes and rub blood into them.
That I am. That once upon a time I was.

2 *Enrico Dandolo's Tombstone*

Blind magician, stop-at-nothing boss,
maestro of the Adriatic. You caustic
tongue-twister, you ancient extractor,
levelled at last on this disputed ground
– crosses and candles, six-lobed coronas –
underfoot at the feet of your only Master
and the flashing mosaic you never saw.

Byzantium's sons dismembered you,
and her avenging daughters threw
their mongrels your old bones.
Today and yesterday and tomorrow...
Down, down again, stammering down
from the dark-eyed dome: feather-flames
still writhing over your unquiet tomb.

Puzzling

A god and yet a man?
A virgin yet a mother:
Mind puzzles what mind can
Conceive either wonder.

A god, how can he die?
A dead man, can he live?
How can mind reply?
What reason reason give?

The Holy Gospels testify it.
But man's mind is too muzzled
By reason to divine it.
Have faith. Stop puzzling.

Wellspring

At the wellspring under a blackthorn
You could be healed not long ago.
Now beside it a virgin stands
Flowing with love, bound and forlorn.
Whosoever longs for true love,
It's through her you'll be reborn.

Life-Wells

Jesus' wounds, gaping wide,
Are life-wells for the faithful
– That stream gushing from his side
On the cross at Calvary.

If you long to drink
And to escape the fiends of hell,
Kneel down at the brink
And sip meekly from the well.

The Holy Sacrament

It looks white and is red,
It is quick and looks dead,
It is flesh and looks like bread,
It is one and seems to be two.
Christ's body, given for you.

The Corpus Christi Carol

Lulli, lullay, lulli, lullay,
The falcon has swept my mate away.

He swept him up, he swept him down,
And into an orchard wasted and brown.

In that orchard there was a hall
With purple hangings on each wall.

And in that hall there was a bed
With gold hangings burning red.

And in that bed there lies a knight,
His wounds bleeding by day and night.

Beside that bed a maiden prays,
And she grieves both night and day.

And beside that bed there stands a stone,
Corpus Christi engraved thereon.

THE ROSES OF CAMON

Afin que vif et mort ton corps ne soit que roses

Who was she, Madame Alfred Carrière?
Aromatic as linen newly pressed,
Sprinkled with citrus. Zéphirine Drouhin,
So pink and pretty and small, so intense?
And Madame Isaac Pereire? Musky.
Almost her own dish of pot-pourri.
Yolande d'Aragon? Where are they now?
Gone to ground, all of them, in this bitter season.
New Dawn and Buff Beauty, Blossom,
Violette, Crimson Glory… they sound
Like top flight fillies, cheek by jowl
With poet and cardinal in these narrow beds.
Ah, dear one, *Allons voir si la rose*
Que ce matin avoit desclose
Sa robe de pourpre au Soleil,
A point perdu ceste vesprée
Les plis de sa robe pourprée
Et son teint au vostre pareil.

1825! 1840. '78… '80… 1895.
Here they are, this gathering, whose donors
Preferred circling seasons to the perpetual,
Freezing stars, avenues of planes or poplars,
Or cobbled streets in Old Towns.
Look! Loved ones, heroes and heroines,
Muses, memorials, imports, late arrivals,
Even descendants of the hardy stock
Farmers planted one thousand years ago
To gauge the health of their hillside vines –
Bare roots jostling beside the river,
All spit-and-hurtle, and the leaping railway bridge.
Las, voyez comme en peu d'espace

Ah, dear one, *elle a dessus la place*
Las! las ses beautez laissé cheoir!
Not for you the exotic (say, King of Siam)
Or the *Almanach de Gotha* (Crown Princess Margareta)
Or lush Rhapsody in Blue. Not the winged one
Or the wimpled, blurred with her own incense,
Not even the improbable Threepenny Bit.
Your favourite was the single Cocktail,
village cousin of the ramping Dog Rose.
True, five or six blooms in each cluster
(Unlike you, an only child), but each of them
So open-faced, so independent.
Upright. Very bright. Yellow and red
And a stamen creamy, deepening to apricot.

You said she was long-lasting and unblinking,
And I thought of you as unafraid, a truth-teller.
Questioning, challenging, always persistent.
You said yes, she was tough-minded.
You said she was prickly, but quite attractive
To bees. Hostile, however, to drones, I supposed.
Strong willed, I thought. Seldom in doubt.
But when you smiled and slightly trembled
I surmised you were laughing at yourself.

How bedded you were in your Suffolk acres,
Affirming your husband and your home,
The cornucopia in your own garden.
With the sheaf of your hair loosely tied
In a golden bun or a harvest bow, you'd arrive
On our doorstep with an overflowing basket.
O *vrayment marâtre Nature,*
Puis qu'une telle fleur ne dure
Que du matin jusques au soir!

Your eye was so sharp. I doubt you ever
Missed a cedilla or circumflex.
Reading… assessing… corresponding
(Your round hand open, that of a young girl)…
You were never a woman so busy with omens
Or the numinous that you failed
To be curious about whatever is:
Age, fabric, detail, sound, tone, design.

White Grootendorst and Renaissance,
Christoph Colomb, Baron Girod de l'Ain
(A true dandy, crimson with a white rim):
In the little courtyards and up flaking walls,
Around two rickety chairs and the drinking table,
– In the stillness of the village and the cloister,
Imperturbable, of l'Abbaye-Château,
All the roses of Camon are rising again.
Belle Hélène de citron et de miel,
They will breathe, breathe and quiver.
In their summer season they will nod and incline.
Ah, dear one, we will remember you.

No longer my sweet throstle, attending the sun's rising. Defying the dusk. Your voice was so parched and husky.

I know who I was . . .

My Gracie.

Scarcely a day I've not talked to you, since you went walking up around the mountain.

Not what may have happened, and what did not happen. The sightings and the hearsay. In his account of the three parishes, Martyn Lewis has recorded all that.

Not the chatter about how with his eye-glass Elijah spied you on the third day 'bouncing down' from the mountain, and you wearing a grey dress and pale green apron. Or how you were seen on the docks at Swansea in the year of Trafalgar. Stuff!

Not the old stories either. Falling in with the Fair Family. 'Just one sip . . . such delights. . . .' Doubting Tom, everyone used to call me that.

No! How our marriage . . . our children . . . the smoke from our chimney . . .

Memories and echoes. Memories and askings. What is time then? And what is memory? What's the use of it? Why do we forget? What is hereafter?

Gracie. You were fifteen.

Scarcely a day . . . And how at last you did come back from the mountain. How you looked as you had looked, so long before. Your skin, apple-blossom. The spring in your step.

I was on my way up to cut the peat.

You were on your way down.

Your tresses, Gracie. Still the same. Barley breaking the red.

Your voice husky. Then so wild, desolate.

Tom!

And before what happened happened. And before the west wind
stooped, and plucked and scattered you.

Again, again and always,

I know who I was. I do not know who I am.

What if this were all true?

Just a couple of beats before the first bar of Opus 21 (C major), Row G
of the burghers assembled beneath the gold-and-white unsmilingly make
room for a petite blonde Minnesotan.

Within touching distance, her old husband sits behind a powder-blue pillar.
He removes his shoes. He presses his soles against the cool tiles.

He's standing close, the old man thinks.

Godfather Death.

Very close.

He is standing between us.

What nonsense, thinks the old man. Godfather Death lives nowhere but
within each one of us.

But then he recalls bargains brokered with Death, deals enabling men and
women to remain a little longer on sweet earth.

They're in the air, he thinks, these stories. The east wind blows them in
from Bohemia. I do not disbelieve them.

The first movement of the first symphony is by now well underway.

Godfather Death is standing so close, the old man thinks.

He turns and smiles at his wife. He's remembering the way only last evening,
only last evening, the daisies shone silver beneath her feet.

The petite blonde Minnesotan reaches out, very firmly she grasps her old
husband's outstretched hand.

At bar 92 (as it later transpires) a grizzled citizen in Row E coughs. He
coughs and gargles. He gargles and he slumps.

Behind him, the burghers and their wives stiffen, and do their very best not
to show they have noticed.

She would not go, the old man thinks, sitting behind his powder-blue pillar.

She would not let me go.

Not yet, no.

What was the bargain?

The old man keeps the beat. With his right forefinger, he gently taps his right kneecap.

Regensburg

ON COMING SECOND

Second fiddle, second best, second rate.
Runner-up: the word itself's an also-ran.

When my mother's father's grandfather
rode third in the Aylesbury Steeplechase
with 'its rattling good jump, 18 feet
of naked water', his neighbours lifted him
on their shoulders, they tossed him
halfway to heaven.
                And to finish fourth
in track or field – out of the medals,
out of the money – is halfway
between exasperation and heartbreak.
Even fifth is very far from ignominious,
while to come last has a certain distinction.
La lanterne rouge, the wooden spoon.
On the green baize after mock O-levels:
GERMAN. CROSSLEY-HOLLAND, K. 3%.
And beneath it, typed in scarlet capitals:
ADVISED NOT TO SIT EXAM.
                  Once you determine
your offspring's no budding Victor Ludorum,
please advocate a completely different tack:
bobbing apples, say, or vowing to enter
the record book with matchbox tops,
or else pursuing the strictly non-competitive:
– a study of natterjack toads in Cumbria,
compound nouns in contemporary verse,
something astral or wholly conjectural.

'Tough! Well tried! Better luck next time!'
I see those damp, lower lips protruding, those
discreet tweed jackets.
                              It's not winning
that matters. Not much. It's not failing.
Second string, second gear, second class!
Runner-up: the word itself's an also-ran.

'Second?' my wife drawls. 'Nothing better.
That's what any proper Lutheran prays for.'

LEFT, RIGHT, FREEFALL, STARFISH

Lying on his left side
he's the monk he dreamed of becoming
during all those chaste weekends
sectioned by bells,
his only sins being to meditate too long
on the penis and testicles of the Cerne Abbas giant
and put one ear to the flimsy partition
while in the watches
Brother John grunted and grew so restless.
True, he took a lively interest
in Old Irish accounts of chastity tests
but rejoiced at courses and conferences
when his allocation was a spare cell,
reminding him of all he did not need
and could have renounced long since,
and he learned faith and doubt
are by no means mutually exclusive.

On his right side
he's grateful not to have been born a woman
distraught at losing her longed-for child,
then muses on how the pursuits of his body
have empowered him, obstructed him
for more than sixty years.
Ah! When passion is so searing
as to be monastic, his limbs
so tangled with hers he no longer knows
which belongs to whom, until she turns away
with a single moan, sated, and ushers
herself into his lap...
He savours the silence,
the final inadequacy of words,

sleeps and enters into the courts of merriment,
until he wakes in the morning smiling
at what he no longer clearly remembers.

Prone,
he crushes his elbows and crotch
and disturbs his troublesome kneecaps.
They all grow Brobdingnagian
and his discomfort soon waylays his thinking.
True, there are those who speak
of hunkering down, and comfort,
and everything being gathered in,
but few of his thoughts are uplifting
and he seldom escapes what he must become:
glinting clods, clay, tilth, ash, mulch.
Face down, he's about to be shot by a masked gunman.
Or else he's on the battlefield,
a man already left for dead.
Chilly, and lying low, he's crouching
like a fearful, flat-eared rabbit,
afraid of suffocating like a baby.

Supine,
he's his boy-self on the top of the bunk again
so close to the pale blue ceiling
he can flatten his palms against it.
And now, listening to the larks
and pressing his palms together
(the head-and heart-line of his working hand
are one and the same) he believes
he will be ready to meet his Maker.

He's as exposed as a yoga master
and knows he always must be.
Immaterial now beneath the roof-tree of the sky,
he could almost float away…
In the Western Isles, he recalls,
a *makar* used to lie on his back to compose.
He placed a large stone on his stomach
and stared into the dark.

SEPTEMBER

I
Sprays of elderberries spilling
out of hedge-windows, pretty not indecorous,
blatant hips, Byzantine eyes
deep-set and misty, these and a copia
of ripe blackberries flanked by tall nettles,
each papula plump and glistening.

Content and consummate, late fruit
are always now-or-neverish.

Coming and going, almost blazing sun
hurries goldfinches to the spilling seeds
of thistle and lavender, and here,
couched amongst ragged, downy heads
stands this perfect clock, a single one,
that has forgotten to tell the time.

II
Waking me, circling the gray horizon,
Lakenheath thunder I mistake at first
for something natural. Rain as fine
as stitching, petit point, silk samplers.
Our garden neither accepts nor rejects it
– blades, petals, leaves all look glassy.

Now, wings thrashing in the thicket!
Piteous piping. Slight scrape of my sandals.

No ambition, no further expectation:
each hour is whey-faced, scarcely
rising. Not even a thimbleful of wind.
Caught in her mauve and pewter
pleats, the garden is listening to herself,
beginning the work of her own grieving.

WHAT SHE PROMISES

As usual
and almost daily as bread
books weigh in,
hundreds of thousands millions
of characters
and silences.

If not from the shop
they slip or squeeze
through the sprung flap
drop and slide on their bottoms
across the honeyed tiles.
Some are involved in a small ceremony
some are blessings banes or bores
but each one uncommon
and singular evidence
even the most trifling.

Matter of the spirit,
surroundings, stomach,
home-grown and far-flung:
after the first quick inspection
– font, weight of paper,
self-effacing stitching
or odourless glue,
how the leaves rustle,
the untold ways books mean –
we set them all aside.
In wonky piles
each waits her turn
some rising
some sinking
as seasons pass
destined always to lie low.

Here's one still pristine
in her soapy cellophane.
Ah! Short or long her time
is bound to come:
After some grievous loss,
or locked in loneliness,
we'll unwrap her promises
– this charm waiting to console
even to heal us,
the secret of laughter.

A QUIET MIND

Disembarrassed of all obligations,
the little rituals, dozens of chores
I require and even cherish,
well away from that lofty place
where hunks of chalk, knapped flint
and pale pink brick make subtle harmonies,

and light flooding from four quarters
quickens the colours of invigoration,
quietens the tones of contemplation;
where, through the study's double door,
I can hear women's voices dovetailing
in the kitchen, the old kettle shushing,

yet sit at the desk rebuked for knowing all of it
not as it is but for what I'm making of it
– a cell, a shield where I leave
the spirit like mud on the doorstep
and there's always something more pressing
than to sit and dream and wait and write:

I crouch at the hearth of your Suffolk house
well within earshot of the German Ocean
but for the huge throat gulping and roaring
and the howitzer of a north-easterly
hurling pellets of hail and snow,
coldest of corn, across the tiled courtyard.

The other rooms are pantry-chill, cellar-chill,
heavy-curtained inside, snow-curtained outside,
but here the heart is simmering with half-said
and unsaid because there's no need to say,
the cracking of vast, slow-burning plane logs,
laughter, the antiphon of old friendship.

One by one I start to jettison dog-eared files:
CURRENT, ACTION, URGENT, HERE AND NOW.
I call to postpone long-arranged meetings,
then make an appointment for a heart
out of tune. I write postcards to bright teenagers,
and order mulch for the wakening beds.

George Crabbe crabbed here, Quilter composed,
Boyd hoisted his canvas, Hill located a peacock.
Here on this cusp of a sandy peninsula
 lay gold and garnets in the graves of Wuffings,
and the *scop* sang: *Relish every thing!*
Make good use of each and every thing!

The lion on your sooty fire-back
opens his jaws; lying flat, the shining bellows sigh.
John Ogilby's on his way from London to Yarmouth
(122 miles, 5 furlongs). Even Guinevere escapes
her unending, stricken dream… What's the point
of memory if not to help resolve us?

Until once again I begin to link words
and discover a story – very far from certain
which way forward, knowing only the gift
is mine to fashion and give what's due back:
come the bright morning when I purr north,
unhurrying, quick to myself again.

THE SYRIAN GODDESS

Sea-monsters, she's seen her fair share of those
– many more than cartographers
fossicking in reading rooms
and poring over unwieldy maps,
their borders crowded with tritons and sea-pigs
and other horrid crossbreeds.

She has even ridden on Leviathan,
he who *maketh the deep to boil like a pot*
and *a path to shine after him.*

But this soft skywater
gathered in the scallops of rocks above the tideline,
soured already,
gone yellow-green and unholy,
and the ocean itself,
oleaginous and sluggish and stinking...

Atargatis lifts her eyes
and stares at herself
throttled between clouds, charcoal, indigo.
She waits for her hour to come
and her heart races,
she thrashes her tail.

Before dawn the sky splits open
and again the dark stars hiss. They whistle and they scream.
They begin to explode.

Mortal and ragged,
from her own children her children shield their eyes.
They kneel and burrow
and stumble through the wreckage.

At the crossing-place, the goddess weeps; she weeps.
Tears of clearest quartz, tears of blood.
She stoops and catches water
in the cup of her hands. She cradles it.

ON THE COCKLE-PATH

It's a kind of steeplechase.
                                        A deep black eye
awaits and the young step straight into it
– a ritual anointing. 'Iodine!'
grandfather says. ' Prophylactic.'
Also, well-nigh indissoluble.
Locals sidestep it, and now and then
some furriner cracks a femur
or tibia.
                        Next, skin-rasping sea-blite
and dozens of pulks tiled with mud mosaic,
Byzantine streams in winding canyons,
the tumbledown bridge decorated
with badges of burned orange lichen.
What is comfortable on the saltmarsh?

A small pool clear as a cloud-window,
fringed with thrift – that's where they're hanging.
Half-in, half-out: just testing the water.
Copper and caramel, blonde, chestnut,
their long hair's unleashed and interwoven
with green strings. Seaweed shoulder straps.
Green satin drapes over their lean limbs,
it slips between their fingertips.
                                        To be mobbed
by mermaids, and favoured with a knob
of sea-lavender, mauve, almost musty.
Whimsical? Wistful? By no means.

These are apprentices, spellbound by boy bands
and Jessie J, up to their necks
in social networking. Two play the guitar,
unaware their combs are plectra.
One has grade VI (harp) with distinction,
another's been to Copenhagen. Of course
they know mermaids and seal-women are magical,
and allow Sheila Disney with her moustache
and webbed feet (she taught them to swim)
may have been the last child of a seal-family.
As for them... Atta-who? Atargatis...
They shrug their tanned shoulders.
                                        They've heard
they can raise storms but not how or why.

They're not freighted with tales or harsh truths
and have yet to learn how their kind kidnapped
poor Hylas.
                   They paint their nails
viridian, and dream boys will fall for them,
but don't mean to wound them or eat them alive,
only to swamp them in their unblinking pools.
They chant as they toss their tears,
but keep dropping them.
                                  Tidal, that's what they are,
lucent, already welling, waves-in-the-gathering.
Saltwaters make and pull around them,
chime and chuckle, and engage with them.

GIRL WITH HAWK

Harebells, scabious, foxglove,
swaying grasses:
she was so slender, so light on her feet,
assembled almost
from Pennine flowers,
but then that's how they sometimes are,
the really tough ones.

On the mica track below Odin's Mine
she stopped and accosted us
and, handsome and dusky,
her Harris hawk
knife-eyed me:
Each life feeds my life
unless she denies me.

'He flew off. Ignored me.
Two miles out across Edale.
I've had one adventure today, I can tell you.'
And then: 'A tiny transistor on his left leg.
He was still hungry
and, praise be, I'd got a few scraps left.'

'His manna,' I volunteered.
'My salvation!
Just bits and bobs, but he's not picky.
My last boyfriend!'
Chestnut and charcoal stripes.
Glaring at me staring at him
jouncing on her right wrist.

'Just joking!'
She gave me such a tearing look
the curious sheep backed off
and turned their butts towards us.
'Been up Mother Hill, then? Seen the earthworks?
They used to eat them, their enemies, they did.
Come on boy! Come on, darling!'

NORTH

Look north more often.
Walk into the wind, your cheeks will blaze.
Find the rough path. Stick to it.
It's shorter.
North is best.
Winter's sky-flames, summer nights' sun-miracle.
Walk into the wind. Climb mountains.
Look north.
More often.
It's a long one, this country.
Most is north.

translated from the Norwegian of Rolf Jacobsen

SNOW AND SPRUCE FOREST

Home. What is home?
Snow and spruce forest
– that's home.

Ours as soon as we draw breath,
ours before anyone names it.
Snow and spruce forest.
And it never, never leaves us.

That drift waist-deep
around dark trees
– it's meant for us.
Its breath mixed with our breath,
it lives unseen within us
and never, never leaves us.
Snow and spruce forest.

Yes, the hill under snow
and tree after tree
as far as the eye can see:
wherever we are
we find our selves facing this.

And with it this promise
about homecoming.
Coming home,
bending boughs
– so knowing what it is
to be where we belong
it flares in us.

And never, never leaves us,
until it's snuffed out
in our inland hearts.

translated from the Norwegian of Tarjei Vesaas

FLEDGLING MAYBE, MAYBE WINGED

Charged with our two-minded Mother Tongue
garnished with adoptions, adaptations
and choice pickings from the lexicon,
unrestricted by academicians and nervous ministers . . .
Wolf and chaste, corn and blood and mourning:
we apportion each full moon her proper name
and the rogue blue does not phase us, and yet
for her winged sister, ethereal fledgling
– windstorms, moonstorms, nothing but dissent.

Black, and Finder's, and Secret, and Spinner's
drawing and twisting us towards our own
destinies: while rock-jawed dogmatists
lock horns with witches and worshippers,
this almost disembodied shape, little more
than the idea of one, runs ahead of herself again
through hurtling clouds, never to be caught
except in some sky-net quivering
with kennings, stars and shining metaphors.

LANDSCAPE

I dreamed a dream of love. And I love love still
But love's no longer this spray of lilacs and roses,
Their perfume thick in the wood where a white flame glows
At the end of all those paths without turnings.

I dreamed a dream of love. And I love love still
But love's no longer this tempest where lightning imposes
Its pyres on castles, and distorts, and disrobes,
Spots the farewell in the square, then vanishes.

Love is the spark of flint at midnight under my tread,
The word no glossary on earth has translated,
Spume on the ocean, this cloud in high heaven.

Everything grows shiny and rigid as it ages,
Streets have no names and ropes no hitches.
Like the landscape I feel myself stiffen.

translated from the French of Robert Desnos

SIX NORFOLK POEMS

1 WORDS

Go back at last to the lost beginning
and you will find them waiting not hidden
strewn among pink stars on the saltmarsh
in shallow scrapes beside the speckled eggs
of the little divebombers and shocking
as drops of blood on the shingle rashes.

In this place you've always known and thought
you knew — beyond the Nod, no further than Missel,
all bindweed bells now, blite, blue-green holly:
pick up your old pointer beneath this torrent
of fervent light, ready yourself again
to winnow and to pitch, and prick out.

2 NELSON COUNTRY

Because this is my childhood staithe?
A matter of identity? Consolation?

I no longer know why I come back
but know this flux is crucial as breathing
and this place so demanding, sometimes harsh
(treacly mud, flint-grey creeks, oozing marsh)
it expects me. It brings me to book.

Each man must do all he can do
and he must say all he can say. Amen.

3 THESE THINGS

The coast road was closed, the death-marsh deserted,
Strewn with magazines, lights, twisted metal,
    And on the foreshore 1000 spirits of the dead
    Gathered then rose in missing man formation.
In sunlight the F-15s aimed far inland, heading
For the rituals and tears at Lakenheath
    While the wild geese flew far out, protesting,
    High over wave-beat and wind-blather.
Ashen in the mourning wind, banded together.
    Flap and palaver, fury and feather.
'These things we do that others may live.'
    Helpless, and facing even worse weather.

4 CLARIFICATION

Sea-coal his wide eyes
burning with blue flames.

Half the night he dances
on his own casts and carbuncles
and climbs far above his station.

Singing it and springing it.
Making it.
No bounds.

At dawn, he rises
through light levels
as bubbles rise.

He almost clarifies

and his see-through shrimps scoot
among leftovers: scurf, froth, weed.

5 *WINTERING GROUNDS*

They're back!
                    Back from the capes
of Greenland, and Spitzbergen, Iceland,
their ranks ragged, frosty-grey arrowheads
and groups of outliers in wavering lines.
What is it so tugs at the heart?
Sheer wonder it has happened again
– the same geese, these same acres –
and, crick-necked on our doorsteps,
the sudden surge of wild longings?
Is it their conversation, so scratchy, terse,
insisting nothing is easy on earth?
Their fierce delight, rounding on a field
of waste potatoes, barley stubble –
or our own, knowing good times lie ahead?

Due north . . .

ignites the horse-chestnut's topmost candle
dances on the saltmarsh with will-o'-the-wykes
opens peat envelopes on the silken beach.
How many wild bees are draped on Norton
tower? Can you see tomorrow?

. . .veering north-easterly

Before I'm an hour older I'll skim over
the solder of the cold German Ocean
and splosh across polders shoulder to shoulder
with strapping women. This creation light!
Let me echo let me rhyme and chime

to brazen Amsterdam.

SEA-DEW

Open your heart to its slow roll
over – this vast spring tide driving
through the bellbuoys and mackerel shallows
from the flares of Forties and wild Viking,
at last first landing on Scolt Head.

White-caps along the foreshore are making merry.

And high on Chalk Hill the lane is milky,
wavy hedges and verges are shining
with sea-dew – foam of quickthorn, wild cherry,
nettles, cow parsley – and descants
and downpours blossoming before the dark.

PRAYER

Pillar of dust kindled by the sun.
Shaft quicksilvered by the swimming moon.

Give me the grasp to apprehend, and
the grace to make light of my understanding

NOTES

Translations. For Dom and Kas.

Miriam. For my first grandchild, born on 16 August 2010.

Trespasses. For Sally, my sister.

Harald in Byzantium. While he was in his twenties during the third decade of the 11th century, Harald Sigurdsson (Hardrada) served in the Varangian Guard. The first verse is for Aygün Catak.

In Hagia Sophia: Varangian Mercenary. Halfdan (Half-Dane) inscribed his name in runes on a high marble balustrade.

Five Late Medieval Lyrics. These verses come from manuscripts in the British Museum, The Bodleian Library, Magdalen College, Oxford and Balliol College, Oxford. R. T. Davies provides helpful comments on them in his critical anthology, *Medieval English Lyrics* (1963) and I have also adopted his witty translation of 'leave to wonder', the last half-line of 'Puzzling'.

The Roses of Camon. Camon is a small village in Aude, celebrated for its many varieties of roses. The verses in French are by Pierre de Ronsard (1524–1585). This poem is dedicated to the memory of Helen Barber.

Grail of Ash. Gracie's words echo those in 'Dai Sion's Homecoming' in *The Welsh Fairy Book* by W. Jenkyn Thomas (1907).

What She Promises. The book in question is Shusha Guppy's *The Secret of Laughter: Magical Tales from Classical Persia.*

On the Cockle-Path. For Jessica Ring.

The Syrian Goddess. Atargatis, widely known as the 'Syrian Goddess', was Great Mother of earth and water. She was depicted as a mermaid.

Six Norfolk Poems. 2 *Nelson Country.* The last two lines echo one of King Alfred's exhortations.

Fledgling Maybe, Maybe Winged. For Polly Ionides.

Sea Dew. The name Rosemary derives from the Latin *hros maris*: dew of the sea. This poem is dedicated to the memory of Rosemary Crossley-Holland.